WILL OF THE PEOPLE

a brexit bedtime story

Sarah x

JOEY

RedDoor

Published by RedDoor
www.reddoorpublishing.com

Text © 2018 Sarah Bee
Illustration © 2018 Joey Everett

ISBN 978-1-910453-50-6

A CIP catalogue record for this book is available from the British Library

Cover design: Joey Everett

Design & illustrations: Joey Everett
www.chumdesigns.com

HE HADN'T REALLY THOUGHT ABOUT IT BEFORE, BUT NOW HE REALISED WHAT THE PROBLEM WAS. AND HE GOT VERY, VERY CROSS.
I WANT BREAKFAST
boo to unelected bearocrats
end bearnifits tourism!!
I DON'T KNOW WHAT I WANT
NOT USUALLY URSINE GUY BUT GEEZ
OUT OR ELSE!
SOMETHING ABOUT BANANAS
I REALLY HATE THINGS
hip hi
URSIDAE ~GO~ AWAE!
WELL GOSH... STEADY ON THERE.

WILL WOULD SET SAIL ON THE HIGH SEAS, LIKE A PIRATE - LEAVING ALL THAT WAS WRONG IN HIS LIFE FAR BEHIND HIM.

AHOY!!!

HAHAHAHAHA!!!

SO WILL WAS VERY HAPPY TO WIN.

BUT DEEP DOWN, HE WASN'T REALLY THAT HAPPY. AND HE ISN'T HAPPY NOW.

THEATRE

WHATEVER WILL WANTS, WILL IS GOING TO GET. BUT THE TRUTH IS HE DOESN'T REALLY KNOW WHAT HE WANTS.

ALL HE CAN DO IS HOPE.

S///GGH...

ANY SPARE HONEY PLEASE HELP THANKS

WILL!
WILL!
WILL!
WILL!
WILL!
WILL!
WILL!
WILL!
WILL!
WILL WILL OUT
BOOOO TO LOSERS
bankruptcy OR BUST.
we'll pick our OWN fruit
GO HARD AND GO HOME
THERE'S NO 'I' IN 'OUT'

SO WHAT WILL HAPPEN TO US NOW THAT WILL IS... ON HIS WAY?

WELL... WE DON'T KNOW.

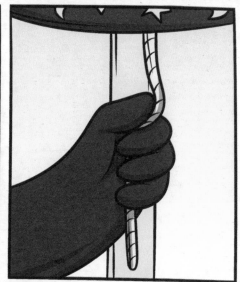

GOODNIGHT, WILL.

This book would not have been possible without these brilliant people, to whom all our thanks:

Sarah Adkins, Neil Atkinson, Chiara Badiali, Sabine Ballata, Ros Banks, Jim Barker, Alex Barraclough, Julian Beck, Richard Bentall, Nicky Bentham, Steve Bradshaw, Seb Brennan, David Brownlee, Lindsay Chapman, Laura Clay, Amanda Cummings, John Dainton, Trevor Datson, Johnny Dean, Linton Dorrell, G S Dove, Pam Dowson, Kate Duggan, Matt Dupuy, Stephen Eastwood, Steve Eleftheriou, Tomas Eriksson, Peter Everett, Simon Everett, Chris Fallon, Rob Fletcher, Tim Footman, David Giles, Caroline Gooch, Clare Griffiths, Oliver Grimshaw, Raymond Halpenny, Steve Harcourt, Will Head, Andrew Hewitt, Ben Hunter, Sammy Ivey, Katie Jenkins, Chris Jennings, Damian Kelly, Laura Kelly, Pierre L'Allier, Gareth Lee, Dominik Lipnicki, Jonathan Livingstone, Wink Lorch, Euan Magill, Alex Maws, Tina Maxwell, Charlie May, Mateusz Łapsa-Malawski, Alastair McAskill, Pete 'Peteches' McCabe, Sarah McCartney, Hari Miller, Julia Morris, Andrew Mueller, David Murthi, Wayne Myers, Craig Myles, Tricia Newborough, Nicos Newman, George Nicoll, Dennis North, Ellis Organ, Beth Parnell-Hopkinson, Doug Robertson, John Robinson, Stuart Ropke, Truls Rostrup, Simon Russell, Théroigne Russell, Nick Sales, Janet Sheppardson, Andrew Stubbs, Jody Thompson, Stephen Trimble, Kristy Tsois, Bob Tyley, Rob Uttley, Samantha Veal, Rebecca Warren, Chris Walker, Rhys Williams, Ben Woodward, Jon Yard, Ed Zed, Robert Zepf & Nikolaus Bernau.

Also **much** gratitude to everyone else who threw in a quid or more to the Kickstarter campaign, shared and retweeted, advised and soothed, and helped to make this book a real thing through sheer encouragement and precious, devalued currency.

Extra-special thanks to Matt (always ursine guy to me), Steve Duffy, Rhodri Marsden, Tim Chipping, Chris & Victoria, Howard David Ingham, Katie Jenkins, Zoe Margolis, A C Grayling, John & Luke at The Quietus, The New European, everyone at RedDoor, Ian Dunt and Adam Kay. And our families. They're just the business.

An absolute absence of thanks to David Cameron, without whom this book would not have been necessary.

Sarah and Joey

@WillMeansBrexit

Sarah Bee is a person from London who has been writing for almost twenty years. Her book 'The Yes', illustrated by Satoshi Kitamura, was the Sunday Times Children's Book of the Week. She has a website, and it is sarahbee.co.uk.

Joey Everett lives in Brighton, and just wants to make things look nice. This is his first book. You can find him at chumdesigns.com.